# Points Of View

Edited by Gemma Hearn

YoungWriters
First published in Great Britain in 2005 by:
Young Writers
Remus House
Coltsfoot Drive
Peterborough
PE2 9JX
Telephone: 01733 890066
Website: www.youngwriters.co.uk



SB ISBN 1 84602 328 9

# Foreword

Young Writers was established in 1991 and has been passionately devoted to the promotion of reading and writing in children and young adults ever since. The quest continues today. Young Writers remains as committed to the fostering of burgeoning poetic and literary talent as ever.

This year's Young Writers competition has proven as vibrant and dynamic as ever and we are delighted to present a showcase of the best poetry from across the UK. Each poem has been carefully selected from a wealth of *Playground Poets* entries before ultimately being published in this, our thirteenth primary school poetry series.

Once again, we have been supremely impressed by the overall high quality of the entries we have received. The imagination, energy and creativity which has gone into each young writer's entry made choosing the best poems a challenging and often difficult but ultimately hugely rewarding task - the general high standard of the work submitted amply vindicating this opportunity to bring their poetry to a larger appreciative audience.

We sincerely hope you are pleased with our final selection and that you will enjoy *Playground Poets Points Of View* for many years to come.

# Contents

# The Poems

## Sea Song

The soft, silent sea has a song to sing
Of pirates, pearls and distant shores;
But also of wind and wild, wild waves
Crashing and colliding with the shore,
As she sings her song of beauty.

Why does the sea ebb and flow?
Why does she show so many moods?
Why does she toss and turn so wildly
And yet lap so gently on the shore?

So often we fail to hear the sea's song
In our troubled world of clatter and noise.
But she's there, always there –
Immortal, immense, alive,
Singing her song of beauty . . .

**Olivia Homewood (10)**

## My Playground

My playground is so cool
My playground is so fun
We all love our playground because it is fun, fun, fun
We play and play all day long in the sun
We have so much fun, fun, fun
When the day is gone we leave the playground nicely.

**Holly Henderson (10)**

## Grandad's Poem

I used to never pray,
I used to say, 'Hip hip hooray!'
Now you have died,
With all my pride,
I say, 'I'll never forget you.'

**Charlotte Lakin (7)**

## Summertime Sizzlers

Summer sizzlers,
Crispy sunbathers,
Paddling with flippers,
Breakfast kippers.

Sandcastle builders,
Hot dog sellers,
Seaside fishers,
Rock pool slippers.

Football players,
Skateboard riders,
Barbecue eaters,
Finders' keepers.

Uniform buyers,
Backpack wearers,
Shoes and blisters,
Teaching teachers.

Tired learners,
Hungry eaters,
TV watchers,
Snoring sleepers.

**Georgia Eardley (10)**

## Recipe For My Creature

Bake a tiger's body for 4 minutes in a hot oven
Chop two frogs legs in 5 pieces
Mix horse legs in a blender for 8 seconds
Roll a lion tail for 10 seconds
Stir dragon wings for 20 seconds
And you have made your own creature.

**Stephanie Ioannou (8)**

## Recipe For My Creature

Mix the zebra's face for 5 minutes and then bake it for 5 minutes and mix it for 5 seconds.
Chop 4 skinny cat legs in 5 pieces
Roll a rabbit mouth twice and cut it
Cook lion paws for 20 minutes and one hour
Boil tiger eyes for 20 hours so they can be hot
And you have made your own creature.

**Rachel Ioannou (8)**

## Recipe For My Creature

Chop the creature's head
Crush the creature's tail
Mix the creature's wings
Cook the creature's hands
Boil the creature's legs
Now the creature is ready to mash.

**Maira Samsudin (8)**

## Sadness

Sadness is like a storm just begun
A little girl that can't find fun,
A horrible place where there's no joy,
Just like when you've broke your toy,
When you are called a horrible name,
Also when you've lost your game,
At the park if you've cut your knee
And when you've been stung by a bumblebee.

**Rosie Ibbotson (11)**

## Happiness

The sweet smell of flowers
The salty smell of the sea
A buzzing of a bumblebee
Happy as can be.
A bright rainbow of colours
A shining yellow sun
Dazzling golden sand
The leaves when spring's begun.

**Hannah Ibbotson (11)**

## Spring

Spring is like silver.
Spring tastes like a very fresh, minty toothpaste in the morning.
Spring reminds me of jumping high.
Spring sounds like birds singing.
Spring looks like a rabbit coming out to play.
*Spring feels like spring!*

**Elliott Bonner (11)**

## In The Playground

*Calm*
There in the sky
Are birds flying
In silence across
The grey clouds.

*Calm*
In the fresh air
There are birds
And a calm breeze
Flies by.

*But not for long*
The doors open and
Reece's running
Lisa's laughing
Katie's kicking
Bethany's bleating
Danny's dancing
Wendy's walking.

*The whistle blows*
All stand still
Jumping, running
Giggling, shouting
To the line.

*Stop, quiet*
We all follow
Into the classroom.

**Ellie Naulls (8)**
**Anlaby Junior School, Hull**

## Playtime

The big, blue sky lay there still
Quiet as a library, oh yes it is
Try to make out a single word or line
But not for long
Smell the air, it smells like roses
Swaying from side to side
But not for long
Because the children come out
Darcy's dancing
Paul's playing
Sally's singing.

**Lauren Stowe (8)**
**Anlaby Junior School, Hull**

## Playground

Soft silence not for long
Whipping wind
Buzzing bees on my knees
With the passing breeze
Not for long
*Ding-dong*
Fred's fighting not for long
Teacher's tumbling
Tanya's telling not for long
David's dancing
Callous kicking not for long
Tom's tattering not for long
*Screech*
Giggling, shouting
Noisy in the line
Quiet
Quiet
*Boom! Boom!*
Door shuts
Silence!

**Jack Burton (8)**
**Anlaby Junior School, Hull**

## In The Playground

Rustling, blowing
In the breeze
Rustling, blowing
Are the trees.

In the playground
Flying around
With no sound
Landing quietly
In your nest.

*But then!*
In the playground
Liam's laughing
Sophie's spinning
Callum's kicking
William's winning
Robin's rushing
Peter's pushing
Daniel's dancing
Bobbie's blushing
*Screech*
Giggling, shouting
Noisy in the line
Quiet! Quiet!
*Boom! Boom!*
Door shuts
Silence!

**Liam Dale (8)**
**Anlaby Junior School, Hull**

## In The Playground

Birds singing
Smells fresh
Not for long
Trees blowing
Men breaking trash
Not for long
Grey clouds waving *bye*
All I see is the dark sky
Not for long.

*When suddenly!*
Glen's grumbling
Yanis is yelling
Teacher's talking
Rachel's running
Macauley's moaning
Darcy's dancing.

*Whistle's gone*
In line
Hollie stop talking
Ellie stop pushing
Poppy stop grumbling

'Please be quiet we're going inside
Playtime is over.'

Quiet again.

**Abbie Mae Raven (9)**
**Anlaby Junior School, Hull**

## Playtime Fun

*Silence around me*
Houses looking straight at me
The wind blowing around me
No screaming and shouting at me
Everything is calm and peaceful around me
Grey clouds above me
Leaves blowing in the air around me
*Connor's chattering*
*Sally's screaming*
*Karl's kicking*
*Frank's fighting*
Playtime is over!

**Emilie Mowforth (7)**
**Anlaby Junior School, Hull**

## Playtime

Creeping, crawling
Lurking around.
Are the birds
That guard our playground.
Towering, swishing
Swaying around.
Are the trees
That look down
On our playground.
Not for long
*Ding-dong!*
Glen's grumbling
Alex's arguing
Paul's playing
Sally's screaming
Gordon's gossiping
Ty's telling tales
Whistle blows
*Toot! Toot!*
Marching in two by two
Then somebody loses
Their shoe
Picking it up
Picking it up
Picking it up
Doors slam
*Boom!*

**Aimee Archibald (9)**
**Anlaby Junior School, Hull**

## In The Playground

The trees sway in the open breeze
As a gasp of wind
Passes by
Silent as a mouse.

A bird flutters by in the open wind
As the grey clouds
Watch in quietness
Silent as a mouse.

As the cars go by
A different coloured car goes ahead
As the seconds go by
Silent as a mouse.

But suddenly playtime starts
William's walking, Tina's talking
Lucy's laughing, Sophie's smiling
Becky's bowling, Daniel's doodling.

People are pushing
People are shuffling
Whispering, talking
Everyone's walking
Trying to get in line
Door shuts
*Peace!*

**Abigail Victoria Hattersley-Gibson (9)**
**Anlaby Junior School, Hull**

## Playtime

Quiet
Grey clouds gliding by
A murky blanket across the sky
Quiet
Trees that in the breeze sway
Blown about on this day
Suddenly
The doors burst open
*Scream*
Dillon's dancing
Liam's limping
*Scream*
Julia's jumping
Caroline's crying
*Scream*
Ty's telling
Kylie's kicking
*Scream*
All of a sudden, the whistle blows
All stand still
Running, jumping, giggling, shouting to the line
*Stop!*
Quiet
We all follow in.

**Jordan Toft (9)**
**Anlaby Junior School, Hull**

## Playground

Quiet in the playground
Grass blowing in the breeze
Trees rustling in the air
Quiet in the playground
Cars running away from us
Grey clouds watching us
Green leaves running past
The flowers swaying all around
Quiet in the playground
Clouds hiding in the sun from us
Quiet in the playground
Rebecca's running
Jessie's jumping
Wesley's walking
Sophie's skipping
Tina's talking
George's giggling
*Bang!*
The doors are shut
End of playtime.

**Hollie Colrein (9)**
**Anlaby Junior School, Hull**

## Playground Poem

Peace in the playground
Trees are swaying in the breeze
Peace in the playground
I hear the buzzing of the bees
Peace in the playground
The cars are passing by
Peace in the playground
The clouds are gliding in the sky
Peace in the playground
The birds are singing from their nest
Peace in the playground
The playground's on a midday rest
Peace in the playground
I smell the petrol from cars
Peace in the playground
The leaves are coming through the bars.

*Suddenly*
Liam's laughing
Fred's fighting
Alex's angry
Bob's biting
Robin's rushing
Peter's pushing.

People are pushing
People are rushing
Standing side by side.
People are chattering
People are nattering
The teacher's marching in pride.

*Bang!*
Goes the door.

**Nathan Lutkin (8)**
**Anlaby Junior School, Hull**

## Before Fun!

The houses staring at the lonely playground
And the noise of the wind but no shouting.
Colourful birds flying in the grey, cloudy sky.
Pity there's no people playing, having fun
And pity there's no blue sky.
But not for long!
Glen's in goal!
Balls are bouncing!
Andy's arguing!
Alex's angry!
Jamie's jumping!
Tom's talking!
Picking it up
Picking it up
Picking it up
Doors slam
*Boom!*

**Becky Snow (8)**
**Anlaby Junior School, Hull**

## Play

The wind is blowing
It's peaceful
The cars are going by
The trees and grass sway from side to side

All the leaves flow by you
The houses are surrounding you
All that makes the noise are the things that go by
All is quiet

The sunlight beams on you
You have to look at it
It's over everything
It makes our shadow
But the door slams
And . . .

David's dancing
Michael's moaning
Connor's calm
Jack's jumping
Danny's dashing
Lucy's loud
The whistle goes
Pushing, stomping, marching in
Crying, screaming, angry going in
And slam
*Silence!*

**Ashley Flannagan (9)**
**Anlaby Junior School, Hull**

## My Playtime Poem

Trees waving farewell
Branches crack
Fall to the floor
Blades of grass swiftly sway
Listen
The abandoned playground
Almost silent
Scattered sticks sway
Football pitch
Like a blank page
The world's switched itself off
Then
*Playtime!*

Doors open
Children charge
Frantic football
Rush around
1, 2
Hide quick
Run around
Block, save all
Where's the ball?
1, 2, 3, 4, 5, 6, 7, 8, 9, 10
Over here
11, 12
Coming, caught you
End of play.

Lining up
Going in
Doors shut
The playground is quiet now.

**Katie Melissa Rust (9)**
**Anlaby Junior School, Hull**

## In The Playground

In the playground
No one there
I can hear
Trees swaying in the breeze
In the playground
Quiet as a mouse
It feels so lonely
You can even hear a woodlouse
People whisper
From school
People muttering
It feels
So cool
*Playtime!*

Luke laughing loudly
Teachers' talking
Harry hopping horridly
Annoying Alex eating apples angrily
Steven shouting slowly
Sam singing stupid songs
Caron cackling carefully
Ted taking teddies
*End of play!*

Shivery
Cold
No one there
Loneliness
*Silence!*

**Alex Withers (9)**
**Anlaby Junior School, Hull**

## The Empty Playground

The breeze of the trees
The movement of the grass
The birds squawking and chirping happily.

The birds zooming past like a sparkle of wind
Look at the leaves gathered all over the playground
Crispy, crunchy leaves clash.

Suddenly, the doors flew open, the children came
Rushing out like a tornado . . .

Helen's hopping
Girls' giggling
Sarah's singing
Whitney's whistling
Sophie's skipping
Jack's jumping
Ben's bouncing
Russell's racing
*Run, run, run*
The whistle blows and the children gather silently
In their lines
In they go
Doors slam
Playground is left
Abandoned again.

**Sophie Wilkinson (8)**
**Anlaby Junior School, Hull**

## Playground Poem

Leaves tingling in the trees
Grass moving like waves in the breeze
Dust pushing through the grass
Little footprints disappear
Basketball hoops still and frozen
Playground empty like a blank page
Feather flying away, away, away
Wind trying to find the way out of the trees
Everything *stops*
Then, *playtime!*

Rebecca's rapping
Pushing, shoving
Amie's jumping
Hopping, skipping
Lucy's wishing she was spinning
Up and down and round they go
James is jogging
Panting, sweating
Thomas is worried
Often fretting
Dale's dreaming
Playing for City
Boys, they like to be the best
*Stop!*

Quiet!

*Peace!*

**Amie Daniels (8)**
**Anlaby Junior School, Hull**

## In The Playground

Cars moving, leaves rolling
Birds singing, trees swaying
Leaves falling off the trees
The smell of grass along the breeze
Grey clouds moving, it smells fresh
The sound of clatter does not matter
Poppy's playing
Liam's laughing
Macauley's moaning
Robin's running
Bobbie's biting
Hollie's hopping
In the playground Chris is chasing
In the playground Becky is bouncing
In the playground Sarah's sad
Jack's jumping
Josh is jogging
In the playground *crash!*
*Doors shut!*
*Peace!*

**Poppy Aitken (9)**
**Anlaby Junior School, Hull**

## In The Playground

Leaves laying lazily on the ground
Listening to the echoes of the children
Trees whisper wisely
Cars communicate
Bees buzz
Football pitch, like an empty page
Bushes moving, like children playing
Plants are waking
World is waking, from a deep sleep
Birds squawking like newborn kittens
Leaves crackling like baby chicks being born
Like the dawn of the world.

*Suddenly,*
The children come shooting out, like a bullet from a gun

Heard it in the playground
I've got a new bike
I've got a new car
Heard it in the playground
I've been to Spain
I've been to Scotland
Well, I've been to France
Heard it in the playground
I've got a new car
Well, I've got a new house
Heard it in the playground
The whistle being blown.

*Stop!*
All the children
Remain silent
The whistle blows
All the children go in
Listen to the echoes of the children.

**Scarlett Alexander (9)**
**Anlaby Junior School, Hull**

## The Empty Playground

I heard it in the playground
I heard cars crackling softly
And the breeze blowing
Like birds flying
I saw leaves blowing on the trees
And I heard the trees rocking
Like twigs scattered across the playground.

I heard it in the playground
I heard cars crackling softly
And leaves blowing
Like flies flying
I saw trees rocking left to right
And children playing about like dogs
Running across the playground.

I heard cars crackling softly
And twigs blowing about
Like fleas jumping
I saw birds flying happily
Across the sky
Like clouds flying above the playground.

I heard cars crackling softly
And children going inside
The whistle went
I was all alone by myself
With silence everywhere
Across the playground.

**Rebecca Stoakes (8)**
**Anlaby Junior School, Hull**

## The Empty Playground

You can hear the lonely creak of the playground
Like an abandoned ghost ship.
Listen carefully.
Leaves are fluttering
You can hear the busy breeze
It's like your tumble dryer blowing.
The dust is dancing deviously
Waiting for playtime.

**Nathan Stowe (9)**
**Anlaby Junior School, Hull**

## Playground Poem

The deserted playground
Was silent and empty
Nobody could hear a thing
Except cars, birds and trees
Swaying left and right.

Ben bumping
Playing football
Firing football
Rodger's rapping
Sarah running sprint, sprint, sprint
Jack jumping
Josh juggling
Helen's happy
Callum's cuddling
Lloyd's laughing
Ty's telling.

The empty playground is deserted
The rain is falling
The wind is floating across the playground
The leaves scramble, scattering with fear
The rain crumbling, *swish, swish, swish*.

**Ben Gemmell (8)**
**Anlaby Junior School, Hull**

## A Playground Poem

Birds tweeting and singing
In the silent, abandoned playground
Leaves swirling like tornadoes
In the silent, abandoned playground
The football pitch is useless
In the silent, abandoned playground.

Suddenly, the bell rings
And the doors *burst* open!

It begins with a trickle of children
Charging, chittering, chattering
Girls walking, talking
Basketballs clattering.

Teachers playing hopscotch
One, two, three
Frantic football players
Pass the ball to me.

Suddenly, the bell goes
The children lead in
The door closes
Listen . . .

Birds tweeting and singing
In the silent, abandoned playground . . .

**Chloe Busby (9)**
**Anlaby Junior School, Hull**

## A Playground Poem

Listen to the trees in the breeze
Listen to the sound of the wind breathing
Listen, it's almost silent
Listen, it's the sound of the world's end
Look at the unused football pitch
Look at the cars rushing by
Look at the scattered sticks
Look, it seems as if the world has stopped.

*Playtime!*
Screaming, stampeding, stomping, shouts
Children chomp, chant, pant
Boisterous boys bash, bosh
I've got a new bike
I've got a newer bike
I've got a bigger bike
I've got a Chopper
I had the chickenpox
So did I! So did I!
Six, seven, nine, ten, so did I! So did I!
Ready or not, ready or not
Run, run, run away
Looking, looking for a stray.

Teacher's coming, looking for you
Teacher's coming, looking for you.

Teacher's coming, looking for *you!*

Whistle blows
Quiet, quiet
*Bang!* The door shuts
It seems like the world has stopped.

**Adam Preston (9)**
**Anlaby Junior School, Hull**

# A Playtime Poem

Calm, gentle trees sway to the rhythm of the gentle breeze
Branches falling, leaves crash together
Squawking crows flutter past
Twigs crawl across the playground like spiders
Grass trembles to the music of the wind
The puddles glisten in the bright, friendly sun
It sounds like the world is waiting for something.

*Suddenly, they all pour out, like a flooded sink!*

Shouting, stampeding, screaming like elephants
Rushing, pushing, shoving, crushing
Boisterous boys are bouncing their basketballs
Thudding, banging, bouncing, bashing
Teachers talking, telling off and tutting
Panting, puffing, jogging, sprinting
*Falling over heads, over heels*
Running, dodging, racing, walking
One, two, three, four, five
Hitting, fighting, smacking, hurting
The whistle blows, everyone freezes
'Silence!' the teacher shouts
Now everyone's in their line
Walking slowly into school
Now the sounds die down again
Leaving everything silent around
The wind howls loudly
And the rain starts to pour
Well, there won't be another playtime today!

**Hannah Murray (9)**
**Anlaby Junior School, Hull**

## The Playtime Poem

The empty breeze pushes me
The playground is like an empty plate
Ready for food on it
In the infants playground
Balls are abandoned
Sticks make it like a bomb
Bench, deserted
Listen to the wind
Look, a leaf has fallen
Listen, infants shouting.

*Playtime!*

Bob's barging
Liam's lobbing
Kyle's kicking
Dan's dodging
Richard's racing
Dale's digging
Carroll's catching
Brian's blocking
Stop!
*Ring! Ding! Ding!*

*End of playtime!*

The playground
Comes back
To its normal self . . .

**Danny Marshall (8)**
**Anlaby Junior School, Hull**

## On The Playground

On the playground, it's silent
On the playground, wind's blowing
On the playground, leaves are rustling
On the playground, nothing to do
On the playground, quiet as a mouse
On the playground, trees swaying in the breeze
On the playground, not even a soul to be seen
On the playground no one to be seen.

Angry Aimee arguing
Lucky Luke laughing
Annoying Alex eating apples
Moody Mona moaning
Happy Harry hopping.

The whistle blows
Everyone stops
The whistle blows again
In they go.

At last . . . *silence!*

**Oliver Cawkwell (9)**
**Anlaby Junior School, Hull**

## On The Playground

In the playground
Silence spreads.
In the playground
Not a soul.
In the playground
Quiet as could be.
In the playground
Not a flea!

Doors open
Noise comes
Footballs moving
No longer peace
And then the teachers come out
Then they start to shout.

When the teachers stop shouting
The whistle blows.
No movement
Whistle blows again.
Into the line
Then into the school.
*Door slams!*

**Alexander Archibald (9)**
**Anlaby Junior School, Hull**

## The Playground

Leaves falling from the trees
The wind whistling
Through my ears
Not for long

It's playtime

Fred's falling
Aimee's angry
Luke's laughing
Darcy's dashing
Shannon's shouting

Whistle goes
Walking, whispering
Pushing in the line
Giggling, stomping
Everybody fine

*Boom!*

End of play!

**Alexander Owen (9)**
**Anlaby Junior School, Hull**

## A Playground Poem

In the playground
Quiet as a pin drop
In the playground
Trees swaying in the breeze
In the playground
Leaves fluttering
In the playground
Birds cheeping
In the playground
Multicoloured butterflies
In the playground
Nothing bothering
*In the playground*
*Year 6 goes in the playground!*

**Alice Watson (7)**
**Anlaby Junior School, Hull**

## The Empty Playground

In the playground the wind weaves in and out of the trees
In the playground the wind chases after the leaves
In the playground trees rustle in the summer breeze
Suddenly, the doors burst open and children run out
Abby's in the playground
Sprinting fast
Run, breathe, run, breathe
Run, breathe, run
Nathan's in the playground
Bullying girls
Punch, smack, punch, smack
Punch, smack, punch
Helen's in the playground
Playing hide-and-seek
Hide quick, hide quick
Hide quick, hide
Bobbie's in the playground
Screaming loudly
Scream, shout, scream, shout
Scream, shout, scream
Everyone's in the playground
Playtime's over, whistle's gone
Quiet
Quiet
Silence
In the playground it's empty once more
In the playground everything's silent
In the playground the wind howls quietly
In the playground the children have disappeared.

**Lucy Murray (8)**
**Anlaby Junior School, Hull**

## The Dead Playground

Look carefully, the breeze gently rustles through the trees
Listen carefully, cars swimming by an abandoned playground.

Look carefully, birds flying calmly through the sky
Listen carefully, birds singing sweetly while they fly.

Look carefully, leaves and twigs lying silently on the playground
Listen carefully, nobody's even whistling.

Look carefully, metal gates float like ghosts
Listen carefully, gates whispering, 'Where is everybody?'

Look carefully, football pitches and game squares deserted
Listen carefully, nobody screams, 'Goal!'

*Playtime!*

Suddenly, children spill out of the door!

Saw it in the playground
I've had flu! Me too! Me too!

Saw it in the playground
I've been abroad! Me too! Me too!

Saw it in the playground
One . . . two . . . three, he's cheating! Four . . . five . . . six!

Seven . . . eight. . . nine, Bill's there! Ten . . . eleven . . . twelve!

I'm coming! I'm coming!
Ready! Ready! Block Jon, block Danny, block Ben, block Joshua.

The whistle blows!
They all get into their lines.
Waiting for the message to go in.
The doors slam shut.
Then suddenly, they vanish, like the wind.
Peace! Playtime's over!

**Stephen Jackson (9)**
**Anlaby Junior School, Hull**

## The Playground

The empty playground
*Ssh!* . . . listen . . .silence
The wind breezes in and out of the trees
Leaves sway in the air
Sticks are scattered like toys
Alone
The empty playground
Useless
Until . . .

*Playtime!*

Alex attacks
Chloe collides
Katy kicks
Ty tidies
Tom tumbles
Sam slips
Jake jogs
Ray runs

Playtime's over
*Ssh!* . . .
Listen . . .
Silence . . .
Empty . . .

**Alexander Jenner (9)**
**Anlaby Junior School, Hull**

## The Playground

The wind is whistling like a soft lullaby - look
It feels like an empty and abandoned room - look
The tree's talking and waving farewell - look
Sticks scattered - look.

All of a sudden . . .

*Playtime!*

Sam is in the playground
Playing football
Children running
Children chanting

Helen's on the hopscotch
Children playing
Running around
Children caring

Tom is in the playground
Fighting children
Teacher's coming
Children fighting

Teacher's coming
Children fighting
Teacher's coming
Children running

Teacher's shouting
Children running
Children running
Children *running!*
Whistle blows
Quiet
*Peace!*

**Freya Chaytor (9)**
**Anlaby Junior School, Hull**

## The Playground

Trees swaying in the breeze
Crows soaring in the sky
Football pitch like an empty page
Scattered leaves moving gently
Grass dancing
Lonely wind swirling
Birds singing songs
*Playtime!*
Out come charging kids
Screaming kids
Charging kids like rhinos
I've got an orange
I've got two oranges
I've got a Mars bar
Look in the playground
Callum catching, Dale dancing
Helen hopping, angry Adam
Kelly kissing, Lewis laughing
Raymond racing
Look in the playground
Jack jumping
Stephen shrinking
Ben barging
Balls bouncing
Girls giggling
Marching in
Doors shut
Peace at last
It is now empty.

**Daniel North (8)**
**Anlaby Junior School, Hull**

## The Abandoned Playground

Leaves scattered like dead bodies
A gentle breeze like a ghost running through the walls
The big deserted playground
Listen
You can just hear the leaves crackling
And the grass dancing
Listen
An abandoned flip chart left out in the cold breeze.

The wind howling
As it weaves in and out of the trees
It sounds like time has stopped!

Suddenly, they come stampeding out!

Boys bouncing basketballs like the First World War
Boys calling, girls stalling
Cheesy children charging around
Now Frank has frowned
Girls doing whirling, whizzing cartwheels
Boys stress, boys barging beastly
Girls screaming and boys steaming
Thomas is tapping
I know Ozzy Osbourne
I have frogs spawn.

Slowly
Slowly
Slowly
Slowly
They go in!

**Raymond Hotson (9)**
**Anlaby Junior School, Hull**

## The Abandoned Playground

First, there's peace,
Leaves scattered, like a flock of birds,
Trees swaying in the breeze,
Crows crowing,
Birds flying from one tree to another, like monkeys,
Then suddenly . . .
Children shoot out, like a bullet from a gun,
Girls doing handstands against a wall,
Boys cheering after scoring a goal in football,
Girls chanting,
Boys yelling,
Girls doing hopscotch,
Boys bashing,
A girl trips,
The whistle blows,
Everyone lines up,
They walk in silently,
The door shuts,
Then, there's peace again.

**Sophie Russell (9)**
**Anlaby Junior School, Hull**

## The Playground

Out on the playground
The trees are swaying
Leaves are crawling
The benches are like soldiers
It's as silent as a hunter
Catching its prey
The football pitch is like a blank page
In a book
Grass is dancing in the breeze
Bikes left in the cold
Bushes as still as a block of ice
It's silent, waiting for . . .

*Playtime!*

The doors open
Heard it in the playground
I've been to France
Teachers talking
One, two, three, block
Kids screaming
Heard it in the playground
Forty-nine, fifty, Carol's crunching
Tom's tooting, basketballs blasting
Ben's behaving, I've been to Liverpool
I've got a truck, ninety-nine, one hundred, block!
The whistle goes
The door
*Slams!*
Then it's back to silence.

**Thomas Dunn (9)**
**Anlaby Junior School, Hull**

## Trickle Of Silence

It all started with a trickle of silence - listen
The birds are tweeting
Leaves shivering, like it is a misty morning
All the branches are scattered.

Suddenly,
*Playtime!*
Heard it in the playground
Have you, have you?

I've got a new bike
I've got a car
I like Mike
I've got a guitar.

One, two, three
Been here
Been there
Ninety-nine, one hundred
Coming, coming, coming
Ready or not!

Basketballs bouncing
Teacher's tutting
Girls gurgling
Harrison hurtling.

Then the whistle blows
And they shoot inside
The trickle of silence begins again.

**Lewis Irving (9)**
**Anlaby Junior School, Hull**

## Heard It In The Playground

It was all silent
Not a word was spoken
All the birds were whistling
The grass was dancing, like honeybees
The wind was blowing, frantically
Suddenly, I could hear children stampeding

Then . . .

*Playtime!*

'I've been to Turkey,'
'I've been to France,'
'I've been to Germany,
I went with Uncle Lance.'

'I've got a new bike,'
'I've got a car,'
'I've got new socks,'
'Well, I've got a bra!'

'Pass me the ball.'
'No!'
'On the head, son!'
'Cool!'

'Give me a fiver!'
'No, give me ten pounds!'

The whistle blew.

Everything was silent as the doors shut
Yet again, I could hear the birds tweeting
Like it was before
It was all silent
Not a word was spoken.

**Alexander Taylor (9)**
**Anlaby Junior School, Hull**

## At Playtime

The football pitches are frozen
Branches are creaking in the trees
Just listen
Everything has stopped
Leaves come fluttering down
It's as slow and silent as a hunter catching its prey
The basketball hoops are empty
You can just hear the wind whistling through the trees
All waiting for . . .

*Playtime!*

Heard it in the playground
I've won the lottery
I've got a dog
I'm going to swimming lessons.

Heard it in the playground
I've got a good gang
I've got a trampoline
Well, I've got a computer.

The whistle goes . . .
The doors . . .
*Slam!*

Everything is silent.

**Ben Parish (9)**
**Anlaby Junior School, Hull**

## Playground Poem

Hear the wind swerving and floating down and down
See the bench stood still like a frozen person
See the canteen stood still like a rocket before shooting up to space
See the branches rocking from side to side
The leaves are floating down off the trees
I look up, I see a tree bigger than me
Like a mountain.

*Playtime*.

It begins with a trickle of children
Kids screaming and shouting
Girls chatting
Girls doing handstands and cartwheels
Girls giggling
Trees swerving
Some balls bouncing and whizzing
Teachers talking and walking around.

**Jodie Morgan (9)**
**Anlaby Junior School, Hull**

## In The Playground

The breeze is blowing through the trees
Sparrows soaring through the sky
The crunchy leaves under my feet
Feathers dancing all around
Grass blowing left and right
Tweet out they come.

Sarah's skipping
Sophie's singing
Scarlett's sleeping
Samantha's shouting
James' jogging
Jack's jumping
Rebecca's running
Danny's dizzy
Dan's dancing
Kelly's kissing
Callum's catching
Louise's leaping
Lucy's listening
Freya's threading
Alan's acting.

*Stop! Ssh!* Listen . . . silence
The playground is once again abandoned.

**Olivia Drydale (8)**
**Anlaby Junior School, Hull**

## Left Alone

Listen carefully
Can you hear the summer's breeze left alone
Looking for someone to play with?
Listen closely
Time has just stopped
Listen
The football pitch is a blank page
When the grass is calm, it floats like the wind itself.

Time can leave you plain alone.

Listen closely . . .

The world has completely stopped . . .

All of a sudden . . .
The doors slam open
It's chaos in the playground
Heard it before
Yeah, yeah, what!
Yeah, yeah, what!
It's chaos in the playground
Balls are bashing
All around
It's chaos in the playground.

Even worse!

Peter's pushing
Stephen's skating
Danny's dodging

But wait . . .
Listen . . .

The playground has just gone dead
And once again alone and at peace.

**Jonathan Tidyman (9)**
**Anlaby Junior School, Hull**

## Playtime

Listen carefully to the summer breeze
Listen carefully to the cars' engines
Listen carefully to the leaves tiptoeing across the playground
Watch closely at the trees swaying in the breeze
Look closely at the lonely football pitch
Look closely at the doors bursting open for . . .

*Playtime!*

Helen's hurting
Sophie's slurping
Katie's kicking
Scarlett's skipping.

The bell rings
We all go in

The lonely creak of the empty playground.

**Katie Osindeinde (8)**
**Anlaby Junior School, Hull**

## Playground Poem

Ten o'clock, emptiness
Feels . . . breezy
Looks . . . strange because *there are no children!*
Smells . . . *like dinner is on the way!*
Sounds . . . *empty!*

Half-past ten . . . *playtime!*
Sandy's singing
Connor's crying
Den's dancing
Tom's talking
Ben's bouncing
Shannon's shouting.

Whistle goes, end of play
*I can hear footsteps and the teachers saying, 'Stop talking!'*

Then . . . *marching indoors*

*Slam!*

*Peace!*

**Kiaya Brown (8)**
**Anlaby Junior School, Hull**

## In The Playground

The nice breeze
Before fun
The trees blow
Before fun
Beautiful leaves
Before fun
On the calm pavement
Suddenly, the doors open
Rosanna's running
Sophie's singing
Sam's skating
Pat's playing
Teachers' talking
Nick's noisy
The whistle goes
And everyone stops playing
They are rushing and running
To get in line
The doors shut
Silence!

**Kerry Hancock (9)**
**Anlaby Junior School, Hull**

## On The Playground

Before fun
Quiet and silence
On the playground
On the playground
The trees are swaying
In the breeze.

Before fun
Green grass
Green trees
Wind blowing
On the trees.

Then the doors open
People shouting, 'Playtime!'
Katie's cartwheeling
Ben's bouncing
Teachers' talking
Helen's hiding
Sophie's skipping
Darcy's dancing.

*End of fun*
Running, giggling
Shoving, grumbling
Whispering, pushing
Waiting for a sign
Going in
End of break
*Bang!*

**Shannon Soltan (8)**
**Anlaby Junior School, Hull**

# A Playground Poem

On the playground the wind whistles along with the breeze
Silence
The trees rattling with the leaves
Silence
You can smell the air
Silence
Fred's frowning
Bill's bullying
Ben's playing hens
Joseph's joking
Luke's laughing
Robin's running
Harry's hopping
Daniel's dancing
*Shush!*
It's end of play
Stop talking
Line up quickly
*Bang!*
Doors are shut!

**Lloyd Pearson (8)**
**Anlaby Junior School, Hull**

## It's Playtime

The trees are swishing
The wind is howling
The birds are singing
The squirrels are rustling
The grass is swishing
The bush is swishing its leaves silently
Not for long
*Ding-dong!*
Kids burst out of the door
Bob's bumping
Jack's jumping
Peter's pushing
Sam's stamping
Samantha's singing
*Ding-dong!*
Back in
Marching in two by two
Someone loses their shoe
Pick it up
Pick it up
Pick it up
Door slams
*Bang!*

**Michael Hall (9)**
**Anlaby Junior School, Hull**

## In The Playground

Silence, the trees are blowing
Silence, the leaves are rustling
The birds are singing and humming
Then Bobby's bullying
Chris is chattering
Hollie is hopping
Jack is jogging
Girls are gardening
Then the whistle blows
Everyone stops
And they run to their lines
Quiet
Quieter
Silent.

**Jack Mulchinock (9)**
**Anlaby Junior School, Hull**

## In The Playground

In the playground
The trees are swaying in the breeze.
In the playground
Leaves are fluttering down.
In the playground
The leaves are scraping across.
In the playground
The wind whistles through the trees.
Suddenly, the doors bang open!
In the playground
Nathan is noisy.
In the playground
Matthew is messing.
In the playground
Rosy is racing.
In the playground
Scott is skipping.
In the playground
The whistle has been blown.
In the playground
Stomping, talking, walking.
In the playground
Lining up, stomping in side by side.
In the playground
*Clang!*
The doors shut.
Silence in the playground.

**Rebecca Hirst (9)**
**Anlaby Junior School, Hull**

## In The Playground

Silence, calm and still in the air
Silence, the green trees waving there
Silence, grey clouds breezily swaying
Silence, brown birds, black birds
Any birds flying
It's playtime
Nathan is nudging
Whitney is walking
Jamie is jumping
Dave is digging
Simon is staring
Whistle goes
End of play.

**Josh Burke (8)**
**Anlaby Junior School, Hull**

## Playground Poem

Ten o'clock emptiness
Feels chilly, empty, deserted
Looks empty, lonely
Smells like food
Sounds quiet
Half-past ten . . .
*Playtime!*
Loud lady Lill
Fred throws a football far
Joe jumps jumpily
Whistle goes, end of play
People walking, silence
Then . . .
Silence, birds squawking, wind blowing.

**James Hoskins (8)**
**Anlaby Junior School, Hull**

## Playground

So silent
The wind is wailing
So silent
A breeze is blowing
So silent
Cars are passing
So silent
Birds are chirping
So silent
Playtime
Ben's banging
Playtime
Sarah's screaming
Playtime
Russell's running
Playtime
Jed's jumping
Playtime
Tim's talking
Playtime
Tim, stop talking
Walter, stop whispering
Peter, stop pushing
Shush, be quiet
We're walking in
Doors are shut
*Bang!*
We're in!

**Jed Pearson (9)**
**Anlaby Junior School, Hull**

## In The Playground

Ten o'clock, emptiness
Feels like spooky
Looks weird
Smells like dinners cooking
Sounds quiet.

Half-past ten . . .
*Playtime!*

Connor crying
Connor coughing
Liam lining
Oliver octopus
Oliver omlette.

Whistle goes, end of play
Line up noisy
Silence.

**Oliver Beardshaw (8)**
**Anlaby Junior School, Hull**

## Outside On The Playground

Still
Winds flowing
Winds blowing
Winds going by
Across the distant sky.

Still
Trees waving
Across the wind.
Trees waving
Side to side.

Still
Leaves rolling
On the ground
Leaves rolling
All around.

And . . .

Ross is running
Emily is eating
Karl is kicking
Jake is jumping
Chloe is catching
Samantha is shouting
Emily stops eating
Ross stops running
Samantha stops shouting
Karl stops kicking
*Bang!*

**Darcy Inch (7)**
**Anlaby Junior School, Hull**

## The Playground

All quiet
Only crows squawking
All quiet
Only wind blowing
All quiet
Blades of grass swaying
All quiet
Sticks scattered
All quiet
Trees swaying above
All quiet
Birds up high
All quiet
Leaves crunching
*Playtime!*
Thomas training
Daniel dozing
Sophie scary
Ben bashing
Wesley wishing
Raymond racing
Everyone freeze!
All quiet.

**James Tock (8)**
**Anlaby Junior School, Hull**

## The Empty Playground

Listen
Closely to the gentle breeze
Listen
Closely to the wind caressing trees
Listen
Closely to the birds calling out to each other
Listen
Closely, it sounds like the world has stopped.

Look
Closely at the flat football pitch laying there, useless
Look
Closely to cars coming past like bees.

*Bang!*
Suddenly, the children shoot out the doors like leopards.

Adam is angry, Ben's bashing
Chloe's caring, Dale's daring
Ellie's eating, Freya's fuming
Gary's gasping, Hannah's hungry
Izzy's whizzing, Josh's jumping
Katie's kicking, Liam's lonely
Mary's mucky, Nathan's naughty
Olli's obedient, Peter's playing
Quill's quirky, Ray's running
Sarah's sinking, Ty's tapping
Whitney's whining.

Look closely, it feels like the world has stopped.

**Joshua Holford (9)**
**Anlaby Junior School, Hull**

## Playtime Poem

Ten o'clock, emptiness
Feels . . . sunny and deserted
Looks . . . strange and huge
Smells . . . dinner
Sounds . . . quiet and peaceful

Half-past ten . . . *playtime!*
Christopher's chasing
Darcy's dancing
Courtney's crying.

Whistle goes, end of play
Stand still, walk and line up.

Then . . .
Single file into school.

**Matthew Hawkings (8)**
**Anlaby Junior School, Hull**

## The Playground

The playground is deserted
The sun is shining on it
The leaves are swaying
Birds tweeting
*Playtime!*
Kids colliding
Helen's happy
Sarah's skipping
Ben's bumping
Jack's jumping
Josh's jiggling
Callum's catching
Kelly's kissing
Ty's tumbling
Finlay's fiddling
Boys barging
Girls giggling
Running rapidly
Footballs firing
Richard's racing
Roger's rapping
*Ding, ding, ding, ding!*
End of play
Whispering
Pole bridging
*Silence!*
Marching in
Doors shut
Peace at last
The empty playground is deserted.

**Jack Bulless (8)**
**Anlaby Junior School, Hull**

## Playing In The Playground

Quiet
The smell of food going by
Quiet
And tiniest bit of sky
Quiet
The sound of clatter
Also does not matter
Then, suddenly,
The door flings open
Yellers yelling
Loud
Poppy is playing
Loud
Macauley is moaning
Loud
Chris is catching
Loud
Liam is laughing
Loud
Bobbie is biting
Loud
Sarah is sorry
*Bang!*
Peace.

**Christopher McFadyen (9)**
**Anlaby Junior School, Hull**

## The Classroom

Busy, busy, busy
Yellow like orange juice
Red to say there's love near you
Purple - as purple as purple can be
Blue so bright it's like the sparkling sea
Books, boring books
The books are over there
Shanice on the computer

Screaming, shouting, silence!
Terrific talking, teachers
Doing their marking

Wonderful warm welcome
Exciting lessons
Phenomenal and fun games at the end of the day

Fabulous fun football
And Cadbury's milk chocolate bubbling in my mouth.

**Ruth Pirie (8)**
**Auchnagatt School, Ellon**

## Classroom

Reading book corner, read
Class stickers, dress smart
Sticker, sticker, sticker chart
Pin board, lots of beautiful things
Work shelf, lots of work, work, work
Trays, trays, lots of things
Tables shiny, brown, hard, wooden tables.

Teacher, talking teacher
Children, chattering children
Pencil writing very fast
People working very, very hard
Reading, reading, reading, fantastic reading.

Happy, very, very happy
Exciting school, exciting.

**Oliver Ormerod (8)**
**Auchnagatt School, Ellon**

## Classroom

Cracking, colourful classroom walls
A piercing red
Blue like a sparkling sea
A beautiful light yellow
A lovely pinky purple
A cracking, colourful classroom
Everyone chatting quietly
Whispering while working
Talking, talking until the teacher says sshh, sshh, sshh.

Superbly successful school
Feeling safe from everything
Stuffy, so hot in our classroom
Cracking, cheerful classroom.

**Alex Paterson (10)**
**Auchnagatt School, Ellon**

## Classroom

Fantastic, fabulous
Fantastic classroom
Super duper, wonderful
Butterfly pictures
Bright, ruby red walls like red-hot peppers
Light blue walls shine like the blue sea
Tremendous yellow like the shiny sun

Chitter-chattering children
Playing all day long
Fabulous, fantastic, tremendous teachers
Telling me what to do
Romantic, tremendous music
Always instrumental
Chalk scrapping along the blackboard

Terribly terrific, tremendous
Relax with wonderful music
Extremely super when I've done all my work in maths
Excited to do something new
Terrific and fabulous when I'm star of the week
Fantastic in maths

Being in a super duper university or college
Fantastic, fabulous, fantastic school.

**Kyle Ormerod (10)**
**Auchnagatt School, Ellon**

## Classroom

Colourful orange classroom like the sunset
Red like a ball of fire
Star chart, glorious golden star
Lots of wicked work on display
As lovely as a beautiful sunset.

Children talking and laughing happily
Tremendous teachers talking to children
Pencils scribbling on the paper
People playing football, screaming.

Fabulous, fantastic and fun
I feel welcome in the class
And phenomenal.

**Sean Troup (8)**
**Auchnagatt School, Ellon**

## Classroom

Blue, blue, mysterious blue
Oh how I wonder about you
The sunshine-yellow lights up the walls
Purple, purple, panicking purple
Red, red, ruby red
Colourful, colourful classroom.

Teachers talking chit-chat
Pencils scratching along the paper
Producing excellent work
Pages turning *swish swash*.

Fantastic teachers working so hard
Phenomenal kids producing great, fabulous work.

**Murray Bremner (9)**
**Auchnagatt School, Ellon**

## Park

Super, successful swings
Successfully sliding down the chute
Phenomenal, fantastic football pitch
Running down the horrendous high hill
Tremendous tall trees and grass
Super successful sandpit.

Bright blue birds chirping
Great green grass being cut
Yelling, speaking, shouting at the referee

Happy, getting a huge amount of space
Excited about what you can do
Relax on the benches
Hot because you have been playing
Fantastic, fabulous, phenomenal feeling.

**Rebecca Pirie (8)**
**Auchnagatt School, Ellon**

## Playground

Super successful football pitch
with dazzling goals
Screeching, swishing
ruby red, bright swings
Children shouting deafening the teachers
talking happily
Feeling happy with joy
and excited at the same time too.

**Jake Smith (10)**
**Auchnagatt School, Ellon**

## Toilets

The girl's beautiful bathroom reminds me of a fish aquarium
Calming, very calming
Also relaxing, really relaxing
Just watching the fish going up and down.

Toilet flushing, lots of noise
Swishing, flushing.

Lots of colours like brown, blue
Black, green, white, pink
Multicoloured like a rainbow.

Bathroom is a happy place
Getting ready for PE
Ready to learn something new.

**Cara Taylor (9)**
**Auchnagatt School, Ellon**

## Park

Fabulous, fun, football pitch
Bright, long, green grass
Huge, rough, prickly trees reaching into the sky
Big colourful swings high as the sky

Shouting, chatting, laughter of the children
Buzzing, swirling bee
*Tweet, tweet, tweet, tweet,* goes the bird
Flip, flap, flip, flap, goes the butterfly

Happy, fun, lovely, relaxed, playing in the park.

**Lewis Gerrie (9)**
**Auchnagatt School, Ellon**

## The Train

The big, blue train
Was covered in rain
It moved along the rails
Making puffy trails.

The driver was mad
He was very bad
He wore a suit
And he played the flute.

They got off the train
And walked down the lane
As the train went back
It passed the track.

**Lucy Ash (10)**
**Benhurst Primary School, Hornchurch**

## Homework Time

I can see numbers and signs and questions in my head.
I can hear my mum's voice telling me how to work it out
And telling me the answer.
I can feel the paper and the pen in my hand
As I work out the answer on my hand.
I can feel the answer on the tip of my tongue in my mouth,
Trying not to swallow, because I don't want to lose it.
I can smell my teacher's biro
As he corrects my homework - all right.
I can smell the new pack of team points,
As my teacher gets them out to give me one as a little reward.

**Sarah Wingett (10)**
**Benhurst Primary School, Hornchurch**

## My Brother

You are so ugly,
But what can we do?
Everyone says,
You belong in a zoo.
If you look in the mirror,
No doubt it will crack,
Indeed you look better,
When viewed from the back.

The neighbours complain
And they have the right,
When you decide,
To walk out at night,
The reason is simple,
You give them a fright.

They think you're a monster!
A vampire or ghoul!
Perhaps, you're a werewolf,
Mouth wet with drool?
Then they find out,
It's my brother, the fool.

**Charlie Dorrell (11)**
**Benhurst Primary School, Hornchurch**

## School

School can be great,
As long as you're not late.

School can be boring
And the subjects are annoying.

All the boys are rough,
I think I've had enough.

Just a few more days,
Till the holidays.

When school's done,
I'm going to run, run, *run!*

**Emily Grimes (11)**
**Benhurst Primary School, Hornchurch**

## My Love

He makes me smile,
He makes me laugh,
He makes me dance,
He makes me proud.

He's the boy I need to make me live,
He looks at me, I look at him,
He smiles at me, I smile back.

Although he smiled at me, I already know
That he will never be interested in me.

**Laura-Jane Maslin (10)**
**Benhurst Primary School, Hornchurch**

## In The School Playground

I can hear people screaming,
Footsteps on the ground.
I can see people running and kicking the ball
On the football pitch.
I can smell the tuck shop
At the end of the playground.
I can touch the playground floor
With my hand.
I can taste the tuck
Which is fruit and breadsticks.

**Connor Cooper (10)**
**Benhurst Primary School, Hornchurch**

## Dungeons

The slimy room covered in grime,
Has people in there, they committed a crime.
But one filthy scum loves eating rats,
He keeps about nine, no a dozen bats!
The dungeons have bars and they are rusty,
The old people behind them are all crusty.

The battered floor needs a clean,
Battered by people who are mean.
The wall of graffiti has had a bash,
One person got out in a dash.
The cell looks like it's about to collapse,
If the prisoners don't do things right,
They must do 900 laps!

**Luke Woodage**
**Benhurst Primary School, Hornchurch**

## Limericks

There once was a man named Clark,
Who ate spiders just for a lark,
He got quite hairy,
Looked awfully scary,
But spun really good webs in the park.

There once was a man from Hull,
Who had a bull named Tull,
He was almost dead,
When the bull saw red,
So it got locked up somewhere dull.

**Sean Murray (9)**
**Benhurst Primary School, Hornchurch**

## The Race

*Bang!*
The gun goes off
And I forward I run,
Everyone's behind me,
I'm number one!

*Trip!*
I hurtle to the grass,
I try to get up,
They're all behind me,
Can I still win the cup?

*Win!*
I cross the line,
Triumphantly,
Everyone cheers
And I grin with glee!

**Ebele Nwangu (10)**
**Benhurst Primary School, Hornchurch**

## First Day Of School

First day of school, oh no,
But my mum said I have to go.

The monstrous cars,
Make me think it would be safer on Mars.

The other children are much taller,
It makes me feel even smaller.

As I approach the area,
The school becomes bigger and scarier.

I enter the building
And I start to sing.

Somehow, it takes my fear away
And it helps me through the day.

I stand in the hallway with nothing to do,
Am I supposed to be in class?
I haven't got a clue!

I meet a child called Jay
Who helps me to enjoy the day.

Finally, we have to leave,
It's the end of the day,
That's hard to believe!

**Rebecca Millward (10)**
**Benhurst Primary School, Hornchurch**

## Seaside

Was she waving,
Or drowning?
The sea air
Was wafting
In the hot, blazing sun.
The taste of sand
In my sandwich.
'Nan, let me have
An ice cream bigger than my head!'
I touched the sand
It was so hot, my hands got burnt,
Then I felt the water,
So smooth.

**Bethany Humphrey (10)**
**Benhurst Primary School, Hornchurch**

## The Playground

I can smell the fresh air
And see the children running.
I hear the children screaming
And see people chasing them.
I can taste the chocolate,
Melting in my mouth.
I can feel the football
Playing at my feet.

**Murray Baird (10)**
**Benhurst Primary School, Hornchurch**

## Balls, Balls, Everywhere

If you go into the playground
You're more than likely to get hit with a ball
Than fall over
From basketball to football
To tennis, even cricket
These all use balls
Bouncing up and down
All around
On your head
Hitting people in the face
If you're a teacher
And you're outside
You should not bring your tea
It will spill.

**Ben Lowe (10)**
**Benhurst Primary School, Hornchurch**

## The Car

There was a car,
It got smashed with a bar,
It needed first aid,
The driver paid.

The car was blue,
It got covered in bird poo,
I'd like to think,
It didn't stink.

The driver thought,
He had bought,
A brand new car,
That could go very far.

**Sahil Gul (10)**
**Benhurst Primary School, Hornchurch**

## Victim

Look at me, look at me
I was the one bullied.

I walked to school,
Fearing the big bully,
Look at me, look at me,
I was the one bullied.

I left school,
Awaiting the fearful bully,
Look at me, look at me,
I was the one bullied.

I burst into tears,
I suddenly feel depressed,
Look at me, look at me,
I was the one bullied.

**Abdul Lawal (11)**
**Benhurst Primary School, Hornchurch**

## Victim's Poem

I cry each night
I cry each night

For only the day the bully goes
I stay awake and do not sleep
I wish he would stay away
But each night and each day, he stays.

I cry each night
I cry each night

What shall I do, he's there?
Shall I sleep?
No, I can't
Because when I try, I can't, I feel a punch.

I cry each night
I cry each night

It is so sad
My mum is dead
My dad is away and never here
And all I see is a shadow of doubt.

I cry each night
I cry each night
For the waiting of tomorrow
Could it be worse?

**Charlotte Di Palma (11)**
**Benhurst Primary School, Hornchurch**

## My Birthday

My birthday reminds me of stars
Twinkling in the night sky
Waving down on me
I can't stand not having a starry birthday
On the night before the big day
I cannot sleep, I can't wait
Because I see the beautiful stars
The beautiful stars remind me
Of my presents waiting in the car
It's now the next day
I wake up and run to the car
Waiting for the stars to sparkle.

**Jenny Fluin (10)**
**Benhurst Primary School, Hornchurch**

## Happiness

Happiness is like a big smile glaring over me,
Happiness is like the seaside without the sand and sea.
Happiness makes me happy when I'm feeling down,
Well, so do my friends and so do clowns.
Happiness cheers my mum up so she can take me to places,
We've been to France and eaten strawberry laces.
Happiness makes the sun come out,
School begins to be fun and teachers don't shout.
Happiness sends badness away from us
And now everyone can live without fuss.
Happiness lightens up our day,
Happiness is good in many ways.

**Aishat Ibrahim (10)**
**Benhurst Primary School, Hornchurch**

## My Love

She makes me feel like a king
Part of the royal family
When I look at her
Her eyes glitter
And her mouth goes up
And she smiles at me
She is the one
Who I will never forget.

**Albert Moughton (10)**
**Benhurst Primary School, Hornchurch**

## Victim

I am so lonely
I am so lonely

I know what he says
He makes me so sad
Each day I wish him to go
But he always stays

I am so lonely
I am so lonely

I can't get to sleep
Because he is in my mind
I can't escape from him
He lurks from behind.

**Mickey O'Leary (10)**
**Benhurst Primary School, Hornchurch**

## What I Feel Like In The Playground

I can see the balls bouncing all around you.
I can feel the cool breeze nearby.
I can hear girls chatting on the benches.
I can taste the breadsticks floating on my tongue.
I can smell the hot dogs cooking in the kitchen.

**Ellie-May Parmenter (10)**
**Benhurst Primary School, Hornchurch**

## Sports Day

I could see the people racing.
It was putting me off the racing.
The sound was giving me a splitting headache.
I needed to get out of there.
I touched the hot, green grass
And my sweat on my forehead.
I could taste the spring water on my tongue
It tasted like heaven
And I tasted the mouth-watering ice cream.

**James Morgan (10)**
**Benhurst Primary School, Hornchurch**

## Victim

I am so lonely
I am so lonely
Lonely, lonely, lonely.

I have no friends
I have no house
My dog is all I have.

I am so lonely
I am so lonely
I am so lonely.

I live on the street
All on my own
My dog just chews a bone.

I am so lonely
I am so lonely
Lonely, lonely, lonely.

**Matt Duncan (11)**
**Benhurst Primary School, Hornchurch**

## My Idol

He makes me glad
That I'm not bad
I want to be like him
His name is Jim.

He's all mine
He's very divine
I like his six-pack
When he dances.

His eyes are like a star
Shining in the sky
They shoot past on the stage.

**Phoebe Smith (10)**
**Benhurst Primary School, Hornchurch**

## Sunrise

She appears through a corner of Whitehorse Road,
Wearing orangey-red.
She shines fiery in your eyes
And attracts you to your window.

She looks around and finds a child, all wide awake
And watches the houses below.
She sees some curtains open
And makes everyone awake.

*Cock-a-doodle-doo!*

**Mahmudur Rahman (8)**
**Cayley Primary School, London**

## Theme Park

She built a large theme park with colourful rides.
She made a celebration to invite her friends at night.
She wrapped some gifts with paper,
As bright silver as the moon.

She went back to take a glimpse of the theme park.
She saw stone bricks, roller coasters and boat rides
Bright as the stars.

She knew that it would be a great sight.
Her finishing touch was a big swimming pool
Nice and warm like a jacuzzi.

**Farjana Ahmed (10)**
**Cayley Primary School, London**

## Open The Door

*(Based on 'The Door' by Miroslav Holub)*

Go and open the door,
There might be a person who needs help.
'Help me.'

Go and open the door,
There might be a dragon
Who'll take you to a magical place.

Go and open the door,
Your friend might be there
To play with you.

Go and open the door,
Your cousin might be there.

Go and open the door,
Even if there's nothing there for you,
Even if you need to go to the head teacher's,
Even if you are in detention,
At least, open the door.

**Asad Uzzaman (10)**
**Cayley Primary School, London**

## Disco Party

She built herself a disco party,
With moonlight coming through,
With a beautiful disco ball
And a DJ playing music.
She covered the walls in black,
With balls and people and music,
She made the people wonderful clothes,
She made the view so dark and blue
And a lovely mat on the floor.
She made herself a waterfall,
Right next to the disco party,
With wonderful water falling
And a beautiful statue where the water was.
She made fantastic lights,
Which attracted people to watch,
She made some coins,
So people could make wishes
And when they all came back,
They said, 'Thank you, thank you, for the coins.'

**Suma Begum (10)**
**Cayley Primary School, London**

## Football Dreams

He dreams about being in a match,
Kicked about and being in a stadium.
The ball dreams about being in a shop
And getting stocked.
He dreams about being in the final
Of the World Cup 2000, Brazil and Argentina.
The ball's ambition was to go to Real Madrid
And be a part of their football team.
He doesn't dream about being in the bin
And getting punched.

**Azizul Haque (10)**
**Cayley Primary School, London**

# Open The Door

*(Based on 'The Door' by Miroslav Holub)*

Open the door,
There might be a cat.
Open the door,
There might be a tree.
Open the door,
There might be a garden.

Even if there's nothing there,
Even if there's a bull,
Even if your mum's there,
At least open the door for the roses to flutter in.

**Mushfikah Uddin (9)**
**Cayley Primary School, London**

## Go And Open The Door

*(Based on 'The Door' by Miroslav Holub)*

Go and open the door,
See if it leads outside,
Or maybe another room.

Go and open the door,
Feel the light breeze,
Or the warm air.

Go and open the door,
Smell the scent of flowers
And hear the grass dancing.

Go and open the door,
Do you see a person,
Or a cat waving at you?

Open the door,
You might see a bird's eye view,
Or maybe,
A festival going through.

Go and open the door,
Even if there's nothing there,
Let the sunlight be a guest,
At least you will have some fresh air.

**Tasnim S Amin (10)**
**Cayley Primary School, London**

## Happy

A laugh says happy,
A hand says touch,
A river says water,
A cloud says fluff,
A person says feelings,
A turtle says slow,
A flower says pretty,
The sun says heat
An eye says look,
A millionaire says money,
A bin says rubbish,
A sketch says draft,
A pebble says smooth,
A fish says swim,
A pen says write,
A smile says happy.

**Nadia Ali (9)**
**Cayley Primary School, London**

## Midnight

She arrives in a black limousine
Wearing a black suit
Wearing shiny diamonds and gold rings too
Driving past the street way, putting sleep to everyone
Giving lovely dreams out under the grey sky
In the chilly night, making places warmer
12am comes out of her car as she walks along
With footsteps sounding like drums
And her necklace shaking like a shaker
Banging onto her skin, making tapping noises
She whistles a lullaby, putting babies to sleep
As 12.00am is finishing her job
She tap, tap, taps and puts herself to sleep
And makes everyone forget their worries
Through the night as another time comes along
And wakes up very late, but doesn't want to wake up at all.

**Zara Akthar (10)**
**Cayley Primary School, London**

## Go And Open The Door

*(Based on 'The Door' by Miroslav Holub)*

Go and open the door and see if your son is coming.
Go and open the door and see if your son is kidnapped.
Go and open the door and you will go to the next world.
Go and open the door and you will see the world full of snow.
Go and open the door and you will see the world's biggest
volcano erupt.
Go and open the door and you will see your mum is not coming
Even if there is no one knocking on the door.

**Shuyab Alom (10)**
**Cayley Primary School, London**

# Egg

The egg dreams of being in the freezing fridge.
The egg dreams of being inside his own shell.
The egg dreams of being at the shop surrounded by other eggs.
The egg dreams of being on the farm with his mother.
The egg dreams that instead of an egg, he wants to be a chick.

**Farhana Rahman (10)**
**Cayley Primary School, London**

## My Adventure Park

I built myself an adventure park including:
A golden swing,
A talking bench,
A chicken you lays blue eggs,
A magic see-saw
And even little robots,
Seven big rats,
Big, hairy monkeys
And tiny, little horses,
Come and see
My adventure park,
It's kind of like a zoo,
It has too many animals,
But what can I do. . .?

**Hajera Khanom (10)**
**Cayley Primary School, London**

## Hello

The man says hello
The mouth says talk
The cat says jump
The sun says bright
London says bye-bye
The moon says light
The hand says hold
A watch says time
And the woman says hello.

**Tanzima Jahan (9)**
**Cayley Primary School, London**

## Rise

Yellow in your eyes.
Pyjamas come off.
Instead you think of Heaven.
Think of Hell
Because there's fire in it.

You can go all around the world.
To stop.
So it stops.
You go back to bed.

*Rriiiiinnnngggg!*

**Rakib Ahmed (10)**
**Cayley Primary School, London**

## Midnight

She arrives in a train
Wearing a skirt and a top
Coloured blue and red
She wakes everyone for midnight
And makes them watch the stars
High above the sky
She sings a lullaby to make them go to sleep
Day by day by day.

**Thamina Begum (10)**
**Cayley Primary School, London**

## You're Gone!

If you sleep in school
You're gone!
If your homework is at home
You're gone!
If you fail the test
You're gone!

If you shout
Instead of talking
And you run
Instead of walking
You're gone!

If you giggle all day
You're gone!
If you sleep in school
You're gone!

If you don't read
Coral Rumble books
You're gone!

Guess what?
You're gone!

**Saimah Begum (9)**
**Cayley Primary School, London**

## Wild Cat

A cat with claws of steel,
Whiskers like a pointed pin,
Ears like a narrowed tree,
It is a cat of darkness.

Back of a stiff tree,
A tail like a thin thorn,
Eyes like sparkling diamonds,
Paws of soft silk.

Yet, he is a wonder cat.

**Abdul Samad (10)**
**Cayley Primary School, London**

## Wild Cat

A cat with claws of steel,
Whiskers like twisted wire,
The ears, like pins, so pointy,
He attacks you in the dark.

A beast with the braveness of lions,
Not scared of anything,
He swoops and attacks you,
Never disturb him again.

A cat with fur so bushy,
A tail as big as a giant,
A tongue so prickly, like thorns,
One touch and you will bleed.

A beast so hungry and lonely,
Give him a pat and he will be good,
A cat from wild to good,
Please pat him again.

**Tasmina Qaiyum (9)**
**Cayley Primary School, London**

## Wild Cat

A cat with claws of steel,
Tail, as bushy as a bush,
Body, as fat as an egg,
He slinks away in the dark.

Whiskers, as long as a snake,
A lonely cat, sitting on the edge of a bin,
Looking for things to eat,
As dirty as mud.

**Jannath Uddin (10)**
**Cayley Primary School, London**

## The River - Haikus

Rushing down the stream
Splishing, splashing, sploshing fast
Toward the big sea.

Breaking the hard rocks
Destroying everyone's lives
Clashing stones down cliffs.

Getting polluted
Poisoning people and plants
Making humans faint.

Helping plants grow tall
Making their stem and petals
Keeping them alive.

**Kahlill Mason (10)**
**Christ Church Primary School, Brixton**

## The River - Haikus

The river is big
It spreads its wings far and wide
It flows down the stream.

Out the river's mouth
Out the big rapids they go
Through the meanders.

The river is great
Beautiful in every way
Wide and wonderful.

**Kausarat Aborade (10)**
**Christ Church Primary School, Brixton**

## Pollution - Haikus

Polluting is bad
But keeps our planet cooler
So what should we do?

Rivers flow and flow
Only a dam can stop them
Be very careful.

Should we pollute now?
Or should we stop polluting?
What should we do now?

**Riseld Meminaj (10)**
**Christ Church Primary School, Brixton**

## Pollution - Haikus

Dump rubbish in bins
Make the world a better place
So we are all safe.

Chemical dangers
Happen nearly every day
This needs to stop now.

One day this will stop
Before it gets out of hand
Make your decision.

**Lauren Burton (10)**
**Christ Church Primary School, Brixton**

## Here Come The Vikings

Here come the Vikings with their long beards,
Here come the people that everyone feared.

The Vikings were very bad,
Some people told me they were mad.

Here come the people with the swords
Here come the people who were cowards.

Here come the people that invented chess,
Here come the people who made a lot of mess.

Here come the invaders,
Here comes the kings of raiders.

**Nicholas Pereira Da Silva (9)**
**Christ Church Primary School, Brixton**

## At The Funfair - A Conversation Poem

'Which ride should we go on first?'
'Let's go on the roundabout.'
'The roundabout is so funny!'
'So let's go on it then.'
'Have you got any money to pay for it?'
'No, I got no money.'
'Who is going to pay for it then?'
'Why are you a dummy?'
'You were supposed to bring some money!'
'The funfair is closed now!'

**Jasmyn Dang (9)**
**Christ Church Primary School, Brixton**

## Birds

Birds are so nice, they fly in the sky
They do their own thing and sing, sing, sing
With their lovely wings.

I like their feathers,
With the nice weather.
I like their beaks.

**Shaquille Campbell (9)**
**Christ Church Primary School, Brixton**

## The Vikings

The Vikings fight everyone
Here they come with their swords and axes.
The Vikings made their swords very sharp and
When they got it wrong
They get quite angry.

They invented chess and when
They don't win they will break it.
They are ready to fight
They fought countries and were very brave.

It was a blind night and everyone was sleeping
When the Vikings stole gold and silver coins
When the people awoke
They screamed very loudly.

**Olven Kamal (9)**
**Christ Church Primary School, Brixton**

## Space Is So Nice

Space is so nice,
I like it when
I see things
Fly up in the sky.

When I went
Into space I
Saw the moon
When I
Was
Turning
I saw
The sun
It said to
Me, 'Have
You seen
My mum?'

**Hannah Edwards-Finlayson (9)**
**Christ Church Primary School, Brixton**

## A Space Poem

Sun, sun, you're so funny
I can't catch you even if I run, run, run.

Alien, alien, you're so dumb
You tried to catch a dog, but you fell on your bum.

Alien, alien, I don't like you
You're very, very ugly and you smell like poo.

Sun, sun, you're so big
You're way bigger than 90 guinea pigs!

Shooting star, shooting star, you're so fast
I cannot outrun you, you will go straight past.

Firework, firework you can go so high,
You even nearly touch the sky.

Sun, sun, you're so hot
You look exactly like 600 burning pots.

Mr Rocket, Mr Rocket, you're so fast
I can't catch you; you will be 90 miles past.

**Jordan Ogunyemi (9)**
**Christ Church Primary School, Brixton**

## A Silvery World - Haiku

What a snowy world.
Hills are captured by the snow,
Silvery icy snow.

**Savannah Morley-Anzalucca (9)**
**Christ Church Primary School, Brixton**

## Spring - Haikus

In spring, flowers bloom,
The birds are singing sweet songs
In the warm sunshine.

Flowers come in all sizes
Different colours shine
Beauty and divine.

**Laura Sebuwufu (9)**
**Christ Church Primary School, Brixton**

## Mr Bird, Mr Bird

Mr Bird, you have beautiful wings
And you sing like an angel.
You have lovely feathers,
They're so soft in the air
You soar in the sky
You have a small beak
You have sharp talons like an eagle
You fly in the sky when the moonlight's right.

Mr Bird, Mr Bird your name is Fred
Mr Bird, Mr Bird you know lots of words
And you talk about verbs
And you named your son Herb.

**Amy Singer (9)**
**Christ Church Primary School, Brixton**

## My Best Friend

C allum is a good friend
A respectful person
L aughing all the time
L ovely and superstitious
U nderestimated and powerful
M aster at being funny to cheer me up.

**Liam Smith**
**Melbourne Park Primary & Nursery School, Chelmsford**

## Daisy

D aisy is so beautiful
She is always there for me
A nd when I come home from school
She is always there,
I like my dog because she keeps me company
Every day she is so lovely
S he is good to play with
Y ou are a good cuddly dog
And you will be a cuddly dog forever.

**Andrew Pearce**
**Melbourne Park Primary & Nursery School, Chelmsford**

## My Best Friend

As swift as lightning
As fluffy as a cloud
As mischievous as a robber
Who is he?
My little dog, Casper.

**Aidan Moore (9)**
**Melbourne Park Primary & Nursery School, Chelmsford**

## Kitten

Playful
Black and white
Soft, sweet kitten,
Kittie cat,
You are delicious!
Noisy,miaowing,
Black and white,
Soft
Mysterious mystery
Where did you come from?

**Ryan Moore**
**Melbourne Park Primary & Nursery School, Chelmsford**

## My Favourite Person

My favourite person is special to me
She is always as shiny as the sun,
Best friends are we
She's a load of fun.

My favourite person is bold and brave.
She's like a sister to me
She's been my best friend since the day I came,
I'll always be her friend, you see.

My favourite person is really pretty,
She doesn't like wearing frocks
She's got a fat little kitty
With black polka dots.

My favourite person's a mystery
My favourite person is *Stephanie!*

**Louiscia McCleod (9)**
**Melbourne Park Primary & Nursery School, Chelmsford**

## Cute And Fluffy

Round, fluffy white tail
That camouflages in the snow.
A cute, twitching nose,
As she sits and nibbles on some grass.

Big long teeth that munch through food
Beautiful long ears that tickle my nose.

He is never silly, but is cheeky.

Together we always have fun
My best friend called Twitchy.

**Sila Kalkici**
**Melbourne Park Primary & Nursery School, Chelmsford**

## My Favourite Cat

My cat Felix is fast and cute,
He is the best cat in the world,
Sometimes he is weird,
He is a ginger tabby with blue eyes, fluffy.
He purrs a lot,
He is the best cat in the world.
I love him so much
I have so much fun with him.

**Jordan Brown**
**Melbourne Park Primary & Nursery School, Chelmsford**

## Tiger Woods

It's the Open
My favourite sport
Watching you on the television
Makes me excited
Your swing is accurate
Your caddie is so strong
I think you're the best at golf.

**Olivia Howard**
**Melbourne Park Primary & Nursery School, Chelmsford**

## My Best Friend

My best friend is Jodie
Jodie has got a good personality,
She is fun, plays with me all the time
She cheers you up when you're sad or upset.

If Jodie ever leaves, I'll remember her as a sister.
She is brave and always happy.
Jodie is my best friend
Her favourite colours are baby blue and lilac,
Jodie's favourite animals are dogs and rabbits
Jodie is a fun-loving person
She likes literacy and PE, especially rounders.

Jodie is a good singer
Her favourite song at the moment is 'Rock Your Body'
She laughs and laughs until she cries.

Jodie will always be there for me,
I will be there for her too.

Jodie is always going to be my best friend.

**Laura Theedom (9)**
**Melbourne Park Primary & Nursery School, Chelmsford**

## My Pet Lucky

Lucky is my lovely angel
When I am up,
Lucky is asleep,
Lucky keeps waking me up
Could you ever see a cat like him?
Every night I say to him,
'What a lovely kitty you are
You are very purry and very furry.'
I love Lucky.

**Lorna Dunn (9)**
**Melbourne Park Primary & Nursery School, Chelmsford**

## A Friend Is

A friend is like a heart
Never gives up spirit
She is always at my side
We laugh and laugh until
Our hearts stop beating
As you see we are
Friends for life.

**Katie Williams (8)**
**Melbourne Park Primary & Nursery School, Chelmsford**

## My Next-Door Neighbour

My next-door neighbour is a nice person,
She always plays with me.
She always cheers me up,
She knocks for me when I have nothing to do.
I go round every day,
She is really a good friend
We always have a good time
She is called Yasmin.

**Amy Turner (9)**
**Melbourne Park Primary & Nursery School, Chelmsford**

## I Like Roses

I like roses rosy red
In the garden they do spread
They look so pretty
I can see
They are as pretty as can be
Red, pink and purple too
They are as pretty as you.

**Daisy Bonehill (7)**
**St Luke's CE First School, Redditch**

## Summertime

Roses are red, violets are blue
I am roasting and so are you!
When I am roasting and I see you,
I can see the sky and it is blue.
I feel like a sizzling sausage
On a barbecue!

**Tom Heaselgrave (7)**
**St Luke's CE First School, Redditch**

## My Pretty Pony

One pretty pony waiting for me,
When I come to ride her she is pleased.
She gallops in the field till night,
I love to ride her, she is sweet.
She jumps, trots, walks, canters and gallops very well.
*She loves me!*

**Iona Campbell (8)**
**St Luke's CE First School, Redditch**

## Theme Parks!

Theme parks! Theme parks!
Are such fun, they have rides
I love every one! They're
Fun and scary, funky and bumpy.
When I go home I feel dizzy.

**Christopher Knight (8)**
**St Luke's CE First School, Redditch**

## The Witch Girl

All alone on a hillside high,
No one comes when she starts to cry.
Now a pebble, once a pearl
Now an outcast to the outside world.

Tears rolling down her smooth cheeks
She wonders how did it all begin?
Who started it all?
Of course, Paul.

How did the bullying begin?
Bullying is a sin.
In a fair world bullies don't fit
Stop them, stop it.

**Brigid O'Reilly (11)**
**St Mary's RC Primary School, Blackburn**

## Witches' Brew

Eye of newt and toe of frog,
Gut of lizard and heart of dog,
Take a powdered finger and mix it well,
Boil an ancient toenail and a broken snail shell,
Catch a ray of midnight moonlight,
Mix in a sliver of child's freezing fright
Drop them in, stir it up,
Drink it from a silver cup.

Foot of toad and ear of bat,
Wing of crow and tail of rat,
Take a horse's hoof and crunch it up,
Heat the brain of bull and blood of pup,
Cage a liquid of torrential rain,
Add a teaspoonful of dreadful pain,
Boil and bubble, toil and trouble,
Something wicked this way comes.

Tooth of hippo and jaw of deer,
Skin of mole and fine brewed beer,
Take a tongue of snake and melt it down,
Take the fine ermine from a Lord Mayor's gown
Boil the liver of an overgrown rat,
Take off an ox a bucketful of fat,
Put them in, mix it well
A potion from the depths of Hell!

**James Golding (11)**
**St Mary's RC Primary School, Blackburn**

## Dinner Time

Screaming and shouting as children play,
The teacher shouts, we're on the grass
Today is a lovely day,
The whistle blows for woodwind class,
The children run inside,
The whistle blows at half-past twelve
Hurry, it is dinner time.

**Kate Graham & Kathryn Tattersall (11)**
**St Mary's RC Primary School, Blackburn**

## On St Mary's Playground

On St Mary's playground
It's a bit like a dog pound
The children fight
Like dog's bite
And teeth are often found.

On St Mary's playground
It's a bit like a fairground
Toys are found
And not often taken round
To the lost and found.

**Kyle Ward**
**St Mary's RC Primary School, Blackburn**

## Cats

Cats, cats that wear big hats,
Sit on mats dreaming of rats and . . .
At night look at cute black bats who . . .
Play cricket with cricket bats!

**Peter Seal (7)**
**St Vigor & St John CE Primary School, Radstock**

## Skyscrapers And Cottages

Tall,
Huge.
Big,
Cool
That's what you'd call a skyscraper . . .

Small,
Cosy,
Comfy,
Cool
That's what you'd call a cottage . . .

There is one thing the same with both of these places . . .
They're both cool places to live!

**Emily Seal (10)**
**St Vigor & St John CE Primary School, Radstock**

## My Oasis Of Calm

My oasis is natural
It is a creation of nature in all its beauty.
Twisting willow branches surround me
And wise old oak trees stand tall.
All to be seen is a magnificent lake,
With rows of swans, taking over their cygnets.
A gentle breeze falls upon my face,
Refreshing me.
The lush green grass rubs against my feet,
Like a thick doormat, welcoming me to the oasis.
There is no place more peaceful,
Than my oasis of calm.

**Oliver Dürner (11)**
**South Wilford Endowed CE (VA) Primary School, Wilford**

## The Poem That Refers To The Light . . .

This is just to say thank you to the rain, wind and wetness,
They storm down and soak the world.
They exterminate all smiles,
Wetter it's better!

To the thunder, lightning and hail,
They storm down and terrify, smash, scare,
They disperse of joy,
Badder I'm gladder!

To the nightmares,
They storm down,
And haunt the world,
They destroy all dreams,
Screaming I'm gleaming.

6 o'clock and all's cold
8 o'clock and all's cold.

This is just to say thank you
To the light that buries itself,
Deep down in our hearts,
Waiting for the moment,
A single bad thought,
A sudden bad desire,
Warms it,
Burns it,
Floods it with shining light,
Reforms it,
Makes it,
Light . . .

9 o'clock and all's well . . .
9 o'clock and all's well . . .
This is just to say thank you . . .
For the light . . .

**Caitlin Shewell-Cooper (10)**
**South Wilford Endowed CE (VA) Primary School, Wilford**

## The Great Ice Bear

From aeons ago there was a bear, a great white bear
She was a magnificent snow-white bear,
She lived in an icy world,
All smooth, snowy ice
Kept in a cover of strong blizzards
Always.

Her name was the Great Ice Bear
She had a snow-white coat
She had very, and I mean very sharp claws,
She was as strong as the cold,
One hit and you'd be dead!

The Great Ice Bear lived on seals,
Slippery, scrumptious, blubbery seals
One seal kept her fine for ten days!
She would pounce on them when she heard one,
She especially enjoyed seal pups,
They were a bonus!
Soft, juicy and tender.

One year in three, she had cubs,
In a den shed made out of snow,
Her cubs were really cute,
They hardly had time to play!

The Great Ice Bear looked very cute and cuddly
But really was so ferocious, she had to survive the Arctic battle.

**Beth Brown (10)**
**South Wilford Endowed CE (VA) Primary School, Wilford**

# I Will Put In The Box

*(Based on 'Magic Box' by Kit Wright)*

*I will put in the box . . .*
My brilliant display against Clifton All Whites
A kick of a warm foot hitting a cold and faint check.
A translucent and succulent jelly that seems to be in a mind of its own.

*I will put in the box . . .*
The memory of my mad kittens
My national championship win in London
Me playing in the blue sky.

*I will put in the box . . .*
My very first smile
The sound of my powerful shot hitting the back of the net
Touching a fluffy glass cloud.

My box is fashioned from friendship,
Footballs, basketballs and steel bars.

**James Greenhalgh (10)**
**South Wilford Endowed CE (VA) Primary School, Wilford**

## The Storm

The white serenity of the Arctic plains, is broken by a storm
Waves of snow roll and crash onto the icy landscape,
While in the distance, oblivious to everything around her,
A polar bear waits quietly for the storm to pass,
Her cubs snuggle up to her warm body in search of heat,
Out on the plains a male polar bear searches for food
Hungry and lonely he trudges on while wind and snow buffet him
from all sides.
Slowly he walks on until he disappears in the blizzard.

**Jake Allin (11)**
**South Wilford Endowed CE (VA) Primary School, Wilford**

## The Snow Bear On Ice

During the dark winter weather,
The snow bear is hunting in the freezing snow,
Soon spring will come and a new life will begin.

The frosty snow-covered head peeking out of the warm den to see
if there is any danger,

Vast frozen seas and blizzards,
White snow looking like a nice warm blanket,
Glistening icebergs scattered around.

Waiting like a bear should,
By a breathing hole for something to pop out,
Lying lazily, lazily, lazily, waiting patiently,
Patiently, patiently.

Then a seal pops up and the bear goes wild,
He grabs his prey and kills it,
Now it's time to eat.

**Polly Eve (9)**
**South Wilford Endowed CE (VA) Primary School, Wilford**

## The White Beast Of The North

Frozen white wilderness
Cold freezing Arctic storms passing over every day.
Mountains of freezing snow
Petrifying the battleground.
White, furry predator awaits his prey the seal.
Their sharp claws help them to grip on the slippery ice
Their furry paws keep their feet warm
And leaves big footprints in the snow.

**Jack Terry (9)**
**South Wilford Endowed CE (VA) Primary School, Wilford**

## The Horse

Big and heavy, strong and tall
The horse ran free, but not anymore
It's confined to a stable and munches all day
Spends all of its time chewing on hay.

The tack is cleaned
And we're ready to roar
We jump on the saddle
And gallop across the floor.

The horse was big, but now it's small
It ran out of food, so licks the floor
Spends all of its time running away
From predators that it can't keep at bay.

Living in the wild must be scary for a horse
So for comfort, it goes to its mother, of course.

Big and heavy, strong and tall
The horse ran free, but not anymore
It's confined to a stable and munches all day
Spends all of its time chewing on hay.

**Matthew Read (11)**
**South Wilford Endowed CE (VA) Primary School, Wilford**

## The Sun And The Moon And The Stars

The sun is like a glistening piece of treasure
The moon is like a big silver shadow
The stars are like goldfish scales.

**Amelia Lowe (10)**
**South Wilford Endowed CE (VA) Primary School, Wilford**

## My Magic Box

*(Based on 'Magic Box' by Kit Wright)*

*I will put in the box . . .*
The treasure of my dead goldfish
My first full day of life
And my first word.

*I will put in the box . . .*
The laughter of humans
The sound of an exploding firework
And the sight of my budgie.

**Ross Liggins (11)**
**South Wilford Endowed CE (VA) Primary School, Wilford**

## An Australian Limerick

There once was an Australian snake,
Whose mother taught him to bake
He found it quite hard
With the butter and lard
And he didn't know what to make.

**Emma Leake (10)**
**South Wilford Endowed CE (VA) Primary School, Wilford**

## Poor Kangaroo

There was once an old kangaroo,
Who dropped her false teeth down the loo,
She pulled the chain,
But they popped up again,
All wet and covered in tissue!

**Samantha Hopps (10)**
**South Wilford Endowed CE (VA) Primary School, Wilford**

## The Kangaroo Limerick

There once was a kanga called Roo,
Who liked to bounce to the loo,
Before she would crouch,
She would pull down her pouch,
And let out her son, little Boo.

**Sophie Buckland (10)**
**South Wilford Endowed CE (VA) Primary School, Wilford**

## The Hunter

In the middle of winter
Lies a stormy, white wilderness
With an extra ingredient,
It is the most powerful hunter on Earth!
This bear has a keen sense of smell and sight,
The bear waits patiently by a hole -
But it's not just any hole -
It's a seal's breathing hole!
He stops.
He looks.
He listens.
Then cautiously the seal emerges,
Then like a tiger he pounces!
There is no escape, the seal's head is crushed
Inside his sparkling, white-toothed mouth.
That's how easy it is to catch a seal
For a Polar bear,
The fiercest hunter on the Arctic battlefield.

**Adam Rose (11)**
**South Wilford Endowed CE (VA) Primary School, Wilford**

## The White Wilderness

Springtime, life returns to the white wilderness
Miniature mountains of soft and flaky snow
The mother ice bear is searching for danger all around.

Solid winter space, a continually moving world of perpetual darkness
Bitterly cold blizzards and vast frozen seas
Glistening icebergs scattered around
Waiting patiently by the hole 2 hours or more.

Waiting for seal food to poke out its head
One huge swipe from the white paw, dead and gone
Now it's time to eat, polar bears and cubs
Are having a feast.

**Chloe Cosway (10)**
**South Wilford Endowed CE (VA) Primary School, Wilford**

## The Kingdom Of The Snowbear

Through the vast frozen wilderness
The snowbears are emerging from their warm winter dens
With newborn.

Marching in stealth for the
Freezing Arctic battle
Field to feed.

Mothers and cubs head for the frozen
Hunting grounds, while mothers hunt cubs learn
How to survive in these frostbite conditions.

The fierce, white, furry predators are like
Masters of stealth when it comes to catching their prey.

The ringed seals are especially in danger
From the king of the Arctic.

**Ryan Hayes (10)**
**South Wilford Endowed CE (VA) Primary School, Wilford**

## The Journey Home

Jumpidy, bumpidy
Goes the car,
Flumpidy, rumpidy
By the sea we are!

Humpidy, dumpidy
We bump along!
Scrumpidy, lumpidy
It goes all wrong!

Clumpidy, umpidy
The car does drone!
Stumpidy, cumpidy
We all go home!

**Hannah Lisley (10)**
**South Wilford Endowed CE (VA) Primary School, Wilford**

## A Storm In The Forest

Leaves rustle, trees sway
In the whistling wind that softly blows
Through the hedges and around the restless ferns.

Suddenly the sky cracks, the hills glare
The rabbits run for their burrows
The birds flap frantically and the insects dig deep.

Safely tucked away, thunder roars
Like a hungry lion, ready to be dined
Torrential rain lashes down, dispersing the river across the forest
The mighty wind floors the trees like skittles
On and on the storm rushes down its deadly path
The animals shiver and shake in suspense for the storm to pass.

The storm has gone and all is quiet
The forest awakes and looks around in fear
Some friends old and young are gone, the holes are obvious
Sadness prevails, but the sun smiles again
And new life begins again until next time.

**Stephanie Beresford (11)**
**South Wilford Endowed CE (VA) Primary School, Wilford**

## Limericks!

There was an old man called Tim
Who went to his local gym
He got on the scales
He weighed the size of five whales
And started to work out to get trim.

There was a boy called Sam
Who was melted in a pan
He was frying and baking
His head was shaking
All the way to Japan.

There once was a man called Bower
He found he had lots of power
He fell through his roof
He felt such a goof
And ended up in the shower.

**Elliott Ackroyd (10)**
**South Wilford Endowed CE (VA) Primary School, Wilford**

## My Magic Box

*(Based on 'Magic Box' by Kit Wright)*

*I will put in my box . . .*
The greetings of my baby cousin
The sound of my fish waiting to be fed
The touch of a fluffy white cloud.

*I will put in my box . . .*
My first glimpse of meeting my penfriend
The meeting with an alien in a super secret shed
The smell of toast burning.

*I will put in my box . . .*
My very first smile
The voice of an angel speaking to me
The mad noise of the holiday cows.

*I will put in my box . . .*
The 105 steps in Greece
The cool splash of water
The thought of standing with the winning rugby team.

*I will put in my box . . .*
My mum's laughter
The touch of the sparkling moon
And the sound of slimy croaking frogs.
*My magic box!*

**Hannah Richardson (11)**
**South Wilford Endowed CE (VA) Primary School, Wilford**

## And My Heart Soars

*(Based on 'And My Heart Soars' by Chief Dan George)*

The graciousness of the sunrise,
The peacefulness of the rainbow,
The echoes of the jungle,
*Speak to me.*

The antiqueness of the fossils,
The tension of the predators,
The guiltiness of the poachers,
*Speak to me.*

The rigidness of the mountains,
The power of the plague,
The venom of the snake's bite,
*Speak to me.*

The complexity of the web,
The movement of the waterfall,
The sparkle of the snowflake,
*Speak to me.*

**Tom Shewell-Cooper (8)**
**South Wilford Endowed CE (VA) Primary School, Wilford**

## Man U Vs Birmingham

I can see Wayne Rooney about to get tackled by Darren Carter.
I can hear the crowds shouting in my earhole.
I can feel people squashing me in their seats
Then one minute before the match finishes Alan Smith scores a goal
Then all the people squash me so hard I can hardly breathe.

**Aqeelah Ali (8)**
**Stirchley Community School, Stirchley**

## The Frightened People - Haikus

I can see Vikings
I can see people fighting
I can see swords chop.

I can hear shouting
I can hear screaming children
I can hear crying.

I feel very scared,
I feel sad and heartbroken
I feel all alone.

**Bethany Ann Caldicott (9)**
**Stirchley Community School, Stirchley**

## The Viking Attack - Haikus

I can see fighting
I can see frightened children
I can see big swords.

I can hear shouting,
I can hear charging people,
I can hear screaming.

I can smell fire and smoke
I can smell animals' food
I smell people's sweat.

I feel very sad,
I feel frightened and upset,
I feel on my own.

**Hollie Cheatle (8)**
**Stirchley Community School, Stirchley**

## Man U Vs Birmingham City

I can see Wayne Rooney about to get tackled by Darren Carter
I can hear people shouting at the players from their seats
I can feel the rain falling down on my coat and I feel very cold
And in 89 minutes Darren Carter scores and Birmingham win.

**Emma Jones (8)**
**Stirchley Community School, Stirchley**

## The Astronaut

The astronaut walking
Looking up the space
The darkness makes him feel afraid
He goes into the rocket.
No one is inside
A creature shouts, 'Boom.'
And he jumps up and down
He jumps out the rocket
And runs away.

**Benson Cheng (10)**
**Stirchley Community School, Stirchley**

## Burning Longboats - Haikus

People getting killed
Blood splashing everywhere
People are burning.

Longboats are on fire
People crying, 'Help me please.'
I can hear the guns.

Some burning longboats
Houses on fire like wood bark
People are burning.

**Nathan Mitchell (9)**
**Stirchley Community School, Stirchley**

## War - Haikus

People are burning
Blood splattering on children
Longboats are on fire.

Everyone at war
People are going to die
Children are frightened.

Some cows being cooked
The longship will be on fire
Everyone will die.

**Abrar Chowdhury (9)**
**Stirchley Community School, Stirchley**

## Sun

Whenever the sun comes up it shines everywhere
When the sun comes out the day gets bright
The sun makes you feel happy
You can almost hear the sun burning.

**Razina Begum (10)**
**Stirchley Community School, Stirchley**

# In A Rocket

In a rocket your legs
Turn into jelly
In a rocket your food
Comes out of your belly
In a rocket your food
Is smelly.

In a rocket you feel
Like you're going
To turn into a
Pile of mushy peas.

**Syed Hussain (9)**
**Stirchley Community School, Stirchley**

## Rockets - Haikus

I can see rockets
I hear the rockets zoom past
Zoom, zoom, they all go.

I saw a rocket
Boom, boom! It went past my eyes
And I felt something.

Now I have to go
Bye rockets, no more zooming
And no more booming.

**Fatema Parbin (10)**
**Stirchley Community School, Stirchley**

## What Can You See, Do, Feel And Hear? - Haikus

*What can you see in space?*
Drift around in space
Can you see the shooting stars?
Jump on all planets.

*What can you see in space?*
In space it's pitch-black
In space you can see rockets
You see satellites.

*What do you feel in space?*
In space you're not sad
In space you feel all bouncy
You are excited.

*In space you will hear?*
Not like a baby
You will hear the shooting stars
Nothing like daytime.

**Cheryl Gibbs (10)**
**Stirchley Community School, Stirchley**

## Bouncing Astronauts

As I step off the spaceship
I see the twinkling stars,
I go in space to find out
About the different kinds of twirling planets.
I feel petrified but
Excited, because of the darkness.
I hear absolutely nothing
It is totally silent.

**Jessica Pownall (10)**
**Stirchley Community School, Stirchley**

## In Space

In space you feel light
In space it is opposite from white
In space you see rockets blasting past
In space meteors are moving fast
In space it is very cold
In space you might see a wormhole
In space it is quiet as night
In space it is a beautiful sight
In space you see the blazing sun
In space it is really fun
In space I love the suits
In space you have cool boots.

**Daniel Heffernan (10)**
**Stirchley Community School, Stirchley**

## Night

I lie awake, dreading what comes
Hoping not to be met by him
The terrifying ghost of night
I stand searching for the black cape, and red slits for eyes.

He haunts me all of the way through his reign
Which comes every end of the day
He devours my happiness, feeds on my joy
And leaves until dawn feeling as empty as space.

He pursues me to the depths of my mind
Where I can no longer wake
There is no escape, I must wait until the sun rises
Although this phantom is full of surprises.

But up the sun comes
I have been released
The new day has started
And the ghost of the night has been defeated.

**Thomas Brady (11)**
**Woodfield Middle School, Redditch**

## Crazy Rhymes

Mary had a little lamb
She also had a cat
She gobbled up both her pets
And now she's very fat!

Mary had a little cow,
She fed it safety pins.
And every time she milked the cow,
The milk came out in tins!

Jack 'n' Jill went up the hill
To fetch a carton of juice
When they came down,
They went to town,
And their cow had run after a moose!

**Jonathan Howell (11)**
**Woodfield Middle School, Redditch**

## The Wave Of Destruction

Happy people on the beach,
Children playing in the sand.

A dark cloud, the sea is rising to the sky.
People running, screaming, shouting.

The sea rushes into the shore,
Crashing against houses, buildings and people.
Trees pulled out of the ground,
Cars floating down the street.

People rushing to reach high ground,
Below them is devastation.

The waves return to the sea,
Where are the villages?
Where are the people?
Where is the hope?

**Ben Hyde (11)**
**Woodfield Middle School, Redditch**

## 12 Things To Do With A SATs Paper

Use for toilet paper in your loo,
Or give it to another school or two.
Make a paper aeroplane out of it,
Or make a bone to feed your dog.
Sell it to a fish and chip shop for some dosh,
Or give it to your mum so she can use it as cloth.
Make a massive ball and throw it at the teacher,
Or shred it up and use it as hay for your creatures
Give to your baby for a nappy,
Or fill all the holes so it isn't so gappy.

**Emily Husband (11)**
**Woodfield Middle School, Redditch**

## Dark Are The Sirens

Dark are the sirens of the menacing island
Dark are the eyes of Odysseus' enemy
Deep is the calm blue ocean
Deep is the pile of bleached white bones
Sharp is the edge of the sirens' talons
Sharp is their alluring tune.
Tight is Odysseus, tied to the mast
Tight is the tension of Odysseus' crew
Determined are his crew, to fulfil Odysseus' dream
Strong is the scent of the sweet beeswax,
Strong is the song of the dark sirens,
Free is Odysseus and his crew,
Free are the sirens . . .
To kill!

**Jack Watton & Connor Poole (11)**
**Woodfield Middle School, Redditch**

## Dark Is The Island

Dark is the blood of the cruel sirens' hearts,
Dark are the eyes, dark from their hearts.
Deep is the sea holding the terror,
Deep and evil for ever and ever.
Sharp is the rope cutting their hands,
Sharp is the danger, sharp is the fear.
Deep is the cut struck by the talons,
Deeper the cut, deeper the challenge.
Foggy the mist covering the island,
Foggy the sky where which the sirens fly.
Cruel is the murder of the sailors so young,
Cruel to fall, cruel to die.

**Emily Parkes & Danielle Nevitt (11)**
**Woodfield Middle School, Redditch**

## Dark Is The Island

Dark is the island, surrounded by sea
Dark is the sand, wet and slippery,
Silent are the sirens, who have wings instead of arms,
Silent is the sea, moving slowly and becalmed
Heavy are the rocks, large and wide,
Heavy are the clouds, where the sirens fly
Strong are the sailors, rowing with their oars
Strong are the voices, that shake the shores,
Sticky is the wax, which drips from the sailors' ears,
Sticky is the wax, that falls on their beards.

**Laraib Tariq & Zain Jameel (11)**
**Woodfield Middle School, Redditch**

## Nan's Funeral

My lips begin to tremble,
Tears well in my eyes,
But all I wish is that my nan
Can hear my lonely cries.

**Sophie Randall (11)**
**Woodfield Middle School, Redditch**

## Today, Yesterday, Tomorrow

Today, today, Snow White has fled,
She must be hungry, for she hasn't been fed.
It's not my fault she ran away,
I really would have let her stay.
My mirror is calling me, I have to go
It's not my problem, I hope you know.

Yesterday, yesterday I married the king,
I met his daughter, the beautiful thing,
I bought a mirror for a quid,
Then it calls me an ugly squid.
At least my mirror keeps me company,
For the king has died, but I'm still alive.

Tomorrow, tomorrow on an apple Snow White shall feed,
But inside is a poisonous seed.
I will not kill her, but this is this,
Upon her frozen lips an enchanted kiss,
A prince shall come, but then shall flee,
Snow White is dead for eternity.

**Francine Walters & Sophie Randall (11)**
**Woodfield Middle School, Redditch**

## Night

When the sun goes down
Night is coming your way
It's a time of rest and peace
She comes to you and takes you away.

Her gentle face and deep brown eyes
Her long black coat comforts you
She gloats away, her long silvery hair trailing along
She gives you a smile and sings you a song.

She looks after you when you're deep into sleep
And all of the things buzzing in your head she gives to you
When you open your eyes and let out a peep
She goes away until the very next day.
When we are waiting for her to arrive, she comes
She holds out her hand for me to hold.
She floats away into the sky
The golden stars are her home.

As soon as the sky turns black
I go to bed then I turn back
What if she doesn't come today?
But then she appears and listens to me talking in my dreams.

**Rimah Rafiq (11)**
**Woodfield Middle School, Redditch**

## 10 Things To Do With A SATs Paper

1. Use it as toilet paper
2. Make a collage
3. Shred it and use it for straw in a hamster's cage!
4. Wrap up chips in a SATs paper!
5. Or make an aeroplane
6. Flush it down the toilet
7. Feed it to a hungry dog
8. Make it into a ball
9. And chuck it at the wall!
10. Or give it a one-way ticket to *Pluto!*

**Rebecca Newburn (11)**
**Woodfield Middle School, Redditch**

## 10 Things To Do With A SATs Paper

You can . . .
1. Make it into a paper aeroplane
2. Recycle it for you
3. Burn it for school
4. Flush it down the loo
5. Sell it for some shoes
6. Make a nappy out of it
7. Feed it to a hungry dog
8. Or give it to a pig
9. Give it a one-way ticket to Pluto
10. Make it into a ball to play with when you're going home.

**Sophie Parkins (11)**
**Woodfield Middle School, Redditch**

## Alliteration Poem

An acrobatic African apprentice abseiling
A ballistic barbarian bat burning
A cold canary crucially cruising
A disgusting dog deathly darting
An executing elephant exclusively excreting
A foolish fat fairy farting
A great gigantic goat galloping
A haughty hobbly henchman hunting
An inky icy igloo ice skating
A jilly jolly jelly juggling
A kind karate kid kicking
A loony lanky Larry laughing
A moody manky Martian moving
A naughty nutty nuisance nagging.

**Matthew Lindsey (11)**
**Woodfield Middle School, Redditch**

## 10 Things To Do With A SATs Paper

Wrap your chips to eat on the way home
Burn it to heat the school
Put it through the shredder and use it in the hamster cage
Pile them all up and make an igloo for the homeless
Use as toilet paper to save money
Turn it into a collage to decorate the wall
Stuff it down the toilet so Mum doesn't have to go to the gym.

**Charlotte Turner (11)**
**Woodfield Middle School, Redditch**

## 10 Things To Do With A SATs Paper

1. Tear it up and burn it to heat the school
2. Make a paper aeroplane to throw at the teacher
3. Use it to wipe your bum!
4. Wrap your chips in it and throw them at your brother
5. Stuff it down the toilet, just to see your mum get some exercise
6. Shred it and have a snowball fight
7. Roll it up and throw it at your sister
8. Wrap your brother in it and throw him in the sewer
9. Bury it and dig it up in twenty years
10. Leave it with your little sister and a can of spray paint.

**Caitlin Goldsworthy (11)**
**Woodfield Middle School, Redditch**